Fair's Fair

by Leon Garfield

Jackson was thin, small and ugly, and stank like a drain. He got his living by running errands, holding horses, and doing a bit of scrubbing on the side. And when he had nothing better to do he always sat on the same doorstep at the back of Paddy's Goose, which was at the worst end of the worst street in the worst part of the town.

He was called Jackson, because his father might have been a sailor, Jack being a fond name for a sailor in the streets round Paddy's Goose; but nobody knew for sure. He had no mother, either, so there was none who would have missed him if he had fallen down a hole in the road. And nobody *did* miss him when he vanished one day and was never seen or heard of again.

It happened when Christmas was coming on – about a week before. Dreadful weather, as hard and bitter as a quarrel.

Dreadful weather, with snow flakes fighting in the wind and milk freezing in the pail.

1B Anne of Green Gables — Text 2

by J.M. Montgomery

Blythe wasn't used to putting himself out to make a girl look at him and meeting with failure. She *should* look at him, that red-haired Shirley girl with the little pointed chin and big eyes that weren't like the eyes of any other girl in Avonlea school.

Gilbert reached across the aisle, picked up the end of Anne's long red braid, held it out at arm's length, and said in a piercing whisper:

'Carrots! Carrots!'

Then Anne looked at him with a vengeance!

She did more than look. She sprang to her feet, her bright fancies fallen into careless ruin. She flashed one indignant glance at Gilbert from eyes whose angry sparkle was swiftly quenched in equally angry tears.

'You mean, hateful boy!' she exclaimed passionately. 'How dare you!'

And then – Thwack! Anne had brought her slate down on Gilbert's head and cracked it – slate, not head – clear across.

Avonlea school always enjoyed a scene. This was an especially enjoyable one. Everybody said, 'Oh,' in horrified delight. Diana gasped. Ruby Gillis, who was inclined to be hysterical, began to cry. Tommy Sloane let his team of crickets escape him altogether while he stared open-mouthed at the tableau.

Mr Phillips stalked down the aisle and laid his hand heavily on Anne's shoulder.

'Anne Shirley, what does this mean?' he said angrily.

Anne returned no answer. It was asking too much of flesh and blood to expect her to tell before the whole school that she had been called 'carrots'. Gilbert it was who spoke up stoutly.

'It was my fault, Mr Phillips. I teased her.'

Mr Phillips paid no heed to Gilbert.

'I am sorry to see a pupil of mine displaying such a temper and such a vindictive spirit,' he said in a solemn tone, as if the mere fact of being a pupil of his ought to root out all evil passions from the hearts of small imperfect mortals. 'Anne, go and stand on the platform in front of the blackboard for the rest of the afternoon.'

The Shadow-Cage

Text 3   1C

by Philippa Pearce

The little green stoppered bottle had been waiting in the earth a long time for someone to find it. Ned Challis found it. High on his tractor as he ploughed the field, he'd been keeping a look-out, as usual, for whatever might turn up. Several times there had been worked flints; once, one of an enormous size.

Now sunlight glimmering on glass caught his eye. He stopped the tractor, climbed down, picked the bottle from the earth. He could tell at once that it wasn't all that old. Not as old as the flints that he'd taken to the museum in Castleford. Not as old as a coin he had once found, with the head of a Roman emperor on it. Not very old; but old.

Perhaps just useless old…

He held the bottle in the palm of his hand and thought of throwing it away. The lip of it was chipped badly, and the stopper of cork or wood had sunk into the neck. With his fingernail he tried to move it. The stopper had hardened into stone, and stuck there. Probably no one would ever get it out now without breaking the bottle. But then, why should anyone want to unstopper the bottle? It was empty, or as good as empty. The bottom of the inside of the bottle was dirtied with something blackish and scaly that also clung a little to the sides.

He wanted to throw the bottle away, but he didn't. He held it in one hand while the fingers of the other cleaned the remaining earth from the outside. When he had cleaned it, he didn't fancy the bottle any more than before; but he dropped it into his pocket. Then he climbed the tractor and started off again.

1D The Lion, The Witch and the Wardrobe — Text 4

by C.S. Lewis

CHAPTER FOUR

Turkish Delight

"But what *are* you?" said the Queen again. "Are you a great overgrown dwarf that has cut off its beard?"

"No, your Majesty," said Edmund, "I never had a beard, I'm a boy."

"A boy!" said she. "Do you mean you are a Son of Adam?"

Edmund stood still, saying nothing. He was too confused by this time to understand what the question meant.

"I see you are an idiot, whatever else you may be," said the Queen. "Answer me, once and for all, or I shall lose my patience. Are you human?"

"Yes, your Majesty," said Edmund.

"And how, pray, did you come to enter my dominions?"

"Please, your Majesty, I came in through a wardrobe."

"A wardrobe? What do you mean?"

"I – I opened a door and just found myself here, your Majesty," said Edmund.

"Ha!" said the Queen, speaking more to herself than to him. "A door. A door from the world of men! I have heard of such things. This may wreck all. But he is only one, and he is easily dealt with." As she spoke these words she rose from her seat and looked Edmund full in the face, her eyes flaming; at the same moment she raised her wand. Edmund felt sure that she was going to do something dreadful but he seemed unable to move. Then, just as he gave himself up for lost, she appeared to change her mind.

"My poor child," she said in quite a different voice, "how cold you look! Come and sit with me here on the sledge and I will put my mantle round you and we will talk."

The Little Match Girl

by Hans Christian Andersen

It was snowing and the wind grew cold as darkness fell over the city. It was New Year's Eve. In the gathering gloom a little girl with bare feet padded through the streets. She had been wearing her mother's slippers when she left home, but they were far too big, and she had lost them while hurrying across a busy road. One of them was nowhere to be found, and a boy ran off with the other. So now her bare feet were mottled blue and red with the bitter cold.

In her old apron the little girl carried bundles of matches which her father had sent her out to sell, but all day long nobody had bought a single match from her. Cold and hungry, she made her weary way through the city. Brilliant lights streamed from the windows of big houses, where blazing fires crackled merrily in the hearth, and the smell of roast goose hung on the air, for it was New Year's Eve.

The little girl crouched down in a corner between two houses. She drew her knees up to her chest, but this seemed to make her even colder. She was afraid to go home, for she had sold nothing the whole day! Not a penny had she earned, and her father would surely be angry with her. But it was just as cold at home, for the wind whistled through the cracks in the walls and floorboards.

How wonderful it would be to light a match! All she had to do was take one out of the bundle, strike it on the wall, and warm her fingers at the flame. She drew out a match and struck it. How it sparkled and gleamed! How the flames leapt and the flames danced! It seemed to the little girl as if she were sitting at an enormous iron stove with brass ornaments on it. She stretched out her frozen feet to warm them – and the flame went out. Gone was the wonderful stove, and there she sat in the snow with the burnt-out match smoking between her fingers. ▸

The Little Match Girl

She struck another. The match flared up, making a new circle of brightness. The light fell on the stone wall, which immediately became as transparent as gauze. She found herself looking into a cosy room, where a table stood spread with a white linen tablecloth and set with silver, while in the middle steamed an enormous roast goose. The goose leapt out of the dish towards her – and the match went out. She saw nothing but the cold, grey wall before her.

Once again she struck a match, and found herself sitting at the foot of a magnificent Christmas tree. Thousands of tiny candles twinkled on the tips of the green branches, and brilliant paper streamers and tinsel hung down to the floor. The little girl stretched both her hands towards it – and the match went out. The candles seemed to climb higher and higher, until she saw that they were the cold, bright stars above her. One of them fell across the wintry sky, drawing a long fiery tail behind it. Someone must be dying, she thought, for her old grandmother, who had always been so kind to her, had said, 'Whenever you see a falling star, you know that a soul is on its way to God!'

She struck another match. It threw a warm circle of light all round her, and within the bright circle stood her grandmother, smiling gently down on her.

'Oh, Grandmother,' cried the poor girl, 'take me with you please! I know I shall never see you again once the match burns out. You will vanish, just as the warm stove, the roast goose, and the beautiful Christmas tree did!' Quickly she struck the remaining matches, one after the other, for she did not want her Grandmother to disappear.

Never had her grandmother looked so kind. She gathered the little girl into her arms and swept her up to heaven. How bright everything was! Here she felt neither cold, nor hunger, nor fear – for they were with God.

Early next day the people found the little match-girl huddled against the wall, the spent matches scattered about her. She was dead, but there was a smile of happiness on her lips.

'Poor soul, she was trying to warm herself,' the people said; but no one guessed what beautiful things the match-girl had seen by the light of her matches, nor how happy she was with her grandmother that beautiful New Year's morning.

Harry's Mad

by Dick King-Smith

Most people walk down stairs, putting one foot more or less carefully in front of the other, and perhaps holding on to the banisters. Not Harry Holdsworth, oh no, not he!

Long hours of practice had made Harry expert in unusual methods of getting from the upper to the ground floor of the Holdsworths' house.

Some were comparatively simple – sliding down the bannisters for example, or rolling down the stairs, or hopping down them, feet together, one step at a time. Hopping down but missing out every other step was a good deal more difficult, and could be made harder still by doing it with hands in pockets, or even – the real test – with hands in pockets and eyes shut.

Harry only attempted this last combination when something told him it was going to be a very special sort of day.

2B A Stitch in Time — Texts 7 and 8

by Penelope Lively

> 'You've done it again,' he said. 'But I daresay you didn't mean to.'
> 'Done what?'
> 'Frightened the birds away. There was a pair of linnets.' He looked at her with mild irritation, which turned to active exasperation as something about her caught his attention. 'Where on earth did you get that?'
> 'What?'
> 'The grass vetchling,' said the boy crossly, 'stupid.'
> Maria's hand flew to the now wilting flowers in her buttonhole. 'These? I didn't know what they were.'
> '*Only* the rather rare grass vetchling,' said the boy, 'that's *all*. Don't you know this is a nature reserve?'
> 'No,' said Maria dolefully. The grass vetchling felt now as though it were burning a reproachful hole in her shirt.

2C King Arthur and his Knights of the Round Table

retold by Roger Lancelyn Green

> Without stopping to read what was written on the stone, Arthur pulled out the sword at a touch, ran back to his horse, and in a few minutes had caught up with Sir Kay and handed it over to him.
>   Arthur knew nothing of what sword it was, but Kay had already tried to pull it from the anvil, and saw at a glance that it was the same one. Instantly he rode to his father Sir Ector, and said:
>   "Sir! Look, here is the sword out of the stone! So you see I must be the true-born King of all Britain!"
>   But Sir Ector knew better than to believe Sir Kay too readily. Instead he rode back with him to the church, and there made him swear a solemn oath with his hands on the Bible to say truly how he came by the sword.
>   "My brother Arthur brought it to me," said Kay, with a sigh.

Texts 9a and 9b   3A

6, Orchard Lane,
Puddlesford,
Westfield
6.9.99

Dear Jonathon,

I just had to write and tell you about my new pet. It's a dog, exactly the kind you know I wanted: a Japanese Akita. It's absolutely huge, with a dark face and enormous paws. I can't wait to get home from school to play with him and teach him new tricks. He is absolutely beautiful; you would love him.

You will get to see my new dog when you come to stay in October, because Mum has already said that I can have a friend to stay at half term. We can take him out near the lakes; he loves the water!

Oh, by the way, we call him Sam. Anyway, must go, the dog needs feeding!

Love,
Jack

---

18 Orchard Lane,
Puddlesford,
Westfield

Mr. T. Nettleworth,
Environmental Health Dept.
Town Hall,
Westfield
9.9.99

Dear Mr. Nettleworth,

I am writing to complain about the number of dogs left to wander around the banks of our town lake. I was there the other night with my young daughter, when a large dog appeared from nowhere and completely knocked her over! She was shocked but, luckily not badly hurt.

There is a sign by the lake, which states that dogs are not allowed off the leash at the water's edge, but dog-owners are clearly ignoring this. I urge you to come and take a look at the situation yourself.

Yours sincerely,

M. Thompson

The Editor,
Langfield Echo

18, Robin Court,
Langfield,
Herts.
30.10.98

Dear Sir,
I am writing about the ever-present danger to young schoolchildren of parked cars outside my children's school. In spite of the zigzag lines, cars still park as close to the school gates as possible, obscuring the view of pedestrians and blocking the road. This means that when I have to pick up my children from school (on foot, of course!) I am unable to fit my pram through the tiny gap they leave open to me. There have been hundreds of accidents near the school, and it is only a matter of time before someone is killed. All these drivers are mad and should be locked up! All the parents agree with me.
Let's walk to school and save our children!
Yours faithfully,

U. Barrass

A letter from the Editor

Dear Readers,

Our campaign to stamp out illegal parking outside our city's schools has been gathering momentum. Thanks to you, our loyal readers, the council decided, at their meeting last night, to send round a police car, each morning, to the schools with the most severe traffic problems. In addition to this, sets of posters with safety messages are available, free, from our reception desk in the High Street. If you can display one in your window, it will further help our campaign. There will be a public meeting on Wednesday, 11th of November, in the lecture room at the main police station, Burgess Road, starting at 7 pm. This will be your chance to make your views known to the police, local councillors, the road safety department and your local MP. Of course, representatives from the Langfield Echo will also be there.

Together, we are making a difference.

The Editor

Instructions

Text 11

From Liquid Magic by Philip Watson

It is most important to follow instructions carefully and to take basic safety precautions, especially when conducting experiments. This experiment is about "dancing" mothballs.

DANCING MOTHBALLS

Mothballs are quite heavy and would sink in most liquids. But in this fizzy combination of acidic and alkaline substances they will "dance" in an amusing way.

Materials
- 5 or 6 small mothballs
- spirit-based felt-tipped pens
- large, glass jar and water
- 10 tablespoons wine vinegar
- 2 teaspoons sodium bicarbonate
- wooden spoon

1. Colour the mothballs will the felt-tipped pens.
2. Add water to the jar until it is three-quarters full.
3. Add the sodium bicarbonate and stir until it dissolves.
4. Add the vinegar and stir.
5. Drop the mothballs into the jar.

At first the mothballs will sink. Then they will dance upward. This happens because the acidic vinegar and alkaline sodium bicarbonate react to make carbon dioxide gas. Bubbles of this gas collect on the mothballs. The gas, being lighter than water, lifts the mothballs to the surface. There the gas escapes, so the mothballs sink again, and the chemical reaction is repeated.

Laboratory procedure
1. Put on old clothes, an overall or an apron before starting.
2. Read through an experiment, then collect the materials listed.
3. Clear a work area and cover it with newspaper or other paper. Put an old wooden chopping board or cork tile on the work area if you have to cut anything.
4. Take care not to get anything in or near your eyes. If this happens, immediately rinse your eyes in clean water, and tell an adult.
5. Never eat or drink anything unless told you may do so in an experiment.
6. Clean up any mess you make.
7. Wash your hands if you have touched a chemical, and when you have finished an experiment.

3E Spy Letter — Text 12

To whom it may concern,

I do not have much time left, so I am scribbling down this note. Whoever finds this, read it well; it could make you very rich! Don't ask me how I came by them, but I have buried an enormous amount of very valuable Roman coins, not far from the spot where you find this letter. Follow my instructions carefully and you will be wealthy beyond your wildest dreams! Of course I haven't made it that easy — I've jumbled up the instructions; but once you've **unscrambled** them, all will become clear to you!

Here is what you must do:

- Once you have spotted the branch, walk six paces in the direction it is pointing and stop.
- Finally, make sure no-one is looking and dig! The treasure is buried 30cm below ground level and is wrapped in a plastic bag.
- The third thing you must do is make a quarter turn to the left and walk ten paces; you should stop just in front of an oddly-shaped and very heavy rock.
- Secondly, walk 3 large steps in a westerly direction and stop.
- Firstly, find the tree with the cracked trunk and stand to the North side of it.
- After coming to the rock, look up; you should see an overhanging branch which will point in the direction you now should go.

When you have found your treasure, be sure not to open the bag where you stand; you may have been followed! Take the bag immediately to the police and show them this letter. Ask them to get in touch with Professor John F. Partington of the Ancient History Museum and he will come and look at the coins. You will not believe how much they are worth!

You may be asking yourself why I have not claimed the coins for myself — well that's another story. Let's just say that my duties for the government have led me on an unexpected mission and that is why I am relying on you to collect them for me. I assure you, you will be well rewarded, as the Ancient History Museum has been looking for these coins for the last ten years, since their mysterious disappearance.

Don't let me down. Don't let these coins fall into the wrong hands. Good luck! End of message.

Texts 13 and 14

From 'Collection of Poems' by Sylvia Plath, Faber & Faber Ltd

The Mirror

I am silver and exact. I have no preconceptions.
Whatever I see I swallow immediately
Just as it is, unmisted by love or dislike.
I am not cruel, only truthful —

by Sylvia Plath

The Cobra

His marks are honeycomb,
His eyes are like flying saucers,
His ribs stretch like elastic bands.
The curled teeth shining and ready for a victim.
His back patterns are stars in the moonlight.

Sharon Purves

From 'Poetry in the Making', Faber & Faber Ltd

There Came a Day

There came a day that caught the summer
Wrung its neck
Plucked it
And ate it.

Now what shall I do with the trees?
The day said, the day said.
Strip them bare, strip them bare.
Let's see what is really there.

And what shall I do with the sun?
The day said, the day said.
Roll him away till he's cold and small.
He'll come back rested if he comes back at all.

And what shall I do with the birds?
The day said, the day said.
The birds I've frightened, let them flit,
I'll hang out pork for the brave tomtit.

And what shall I do with the seed?
The day said, the day said.
Bury it deep, see what it's worth.
See if it can stand the earth.

What shall I do with the people?
The day said, the day said.
Stuff them with apple and blackberry pie –
They'll love me then till the day they die.

There came this day and he was autumn.
His mouth was wide
And red as a sunset.
His tail was an icicle.

Ted Hughes

From 'A Book of a Thousand Poems', © *Evans Brothers Ltd*

Song of Summer Days

Sing a song of hollow logs,
Chirp of cricket, croak of frogs,
Cry of wild bird, hum of bees,
Dancing leaves and whisp'ring trees;
Legs all bare, and dusty toes,
Ruddy cheeks and freckled nose,
Splash of brook and swish of line,
Where the song that's half so fine?

Sing a song of summer days,
Leafy nooks and shady ways,
Nodding roses, apples red,
Clover like a carpet spread,
Sing a song of running brooks,
Cans of bait and fishing hooks,
Dewy hollows, yellow moons,
Birds a-pipe with merry tunes.

Sing a song of skies of blue,
Eden's garden made anew,
Scarlet hedges, leafy lanes,
Vine-embowered sills and panes;
Stretch of meadows, splash'd with dew,
Silver clouds with sunlight through,
Call of thrush and pipe of wren,
Sing and call it home again.

J.W. Foley

The Pied Piper of Hamelin

Oxford book of Children's Verse, Iona and Peter Opie

Into the street the Piper stept,
  Smiling first a little smile,
As if he knew what magic slept
  In his quiet pipe the while;
Then, like a musical adept,
To blow the pipe his lips he wrinkled,
And green and blue his sharp eyes twinkled,
Like a candle-flame where salt is sprinkled;
And ere three shrill notes the pipe uttered,
You heard as if an army muttered;
And the muttering grew to a grumbling;
And the grumbling grew to a mighty rumbling;
And out of the houses the rats came tumbling.
Great rats, small rats, grey rats, tawny rats,
Grave old plodders, gay young friskers,
  Fathers, mothers, uncles, cousins,
Cocking tails and pricking whiskers,
  Families by tens and dozens,
Brothers, sisters, husbands, wives –
Followed the Piper for their lives.
From street to street he piped advancing,
And step for step they followed dancing,
Until they came to the River Weser,
  Wherein all plunged and perished!

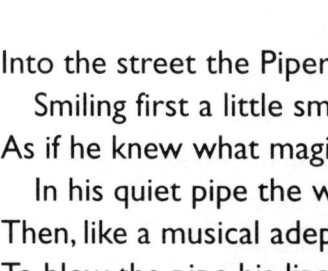

Robert Browning

Isis and Osiris

by Ann Wade

A play in eight scenes, Isis and Osiris is based on an ancient Egyptian myth.

CHARACTERS:
Narrator
Isis (Queen of Egypt)
Osiris (King of Egypt)
Set (Osiris' brother)
Setna (friend of Set)
Thoth (friend of Set)
Horus (Isis' and Osiris' son)
Queen of Astarte of Byblos
King Malcander of Byblos
Malcander's servant
Isis' servant
Servant 1 (of Queen Asarte)
Servant 2 (of Queen Asarte)
Guests at the Banquet
Extra servants

SCENE ONE

The garden of King Osiris' palace

Narrator: Egypt is at last at peace. The people have learned from their God-King Osiris how to use the rich silt of the River Nile to grow crops. There is plenty to eat, fighting has ceased and the people are growing rich. Everyone is content. Everyone that is except Set, Osiris' brother. He is filled with envy for his brother. All he wants is to kill him and seize power for himself.

Enter Set, followed by his friends Setna and Thoth.

Set: I cannot bear to see my brother and his wife so happy. Soon I will be even further from power when their child is born.

Thoth: Why don't you kill him? We could ambush him one night as he walks alone in his garden.

Set: No, it will not be so easy to destroy my brother. Remember he's immortal, so we will need to be very clever.

Setna: Can't he 'accidentally' fall into the River Nile? If we make sure that we put lead weights in the hem of his robes then he will sink to the bed of the Nile quickly. No-one will be able to lift him to safety until it is too late.

Set: It's a good plan and were my brother not a god it would work. No, the only way we can succeed is for Osiris to willingly give up his life.

Silently the men walk together, deep in thought. The cutting of stone is heard offstage.

5B Morgan's Field

by Berlie Doherty

SCENE THREE

Young Morgan: Father! Wait!

Elen: Yes, Cai, we must rest here. I can't go any further. And besides, our people are miles behind us. Look where they are still, struggling down from the misty hills. I think we should wait here for them.

Cai: There's no time to wait. No time to stop, I tell you. My time is short enough.

Olwen: It would be good to rest here. It's so sheltered.

Cai: My time is short enough. I dare not rest until I have found the right place for us to live in.

Elen: But we've been walking now for weeks. Is there to be no rest for us, ever?

Young Morgan: Father! Why don't we stop here?

Cai: I've told you…

Young Morgan: Not to rest, Father! To live!

Cai: To live! Here! You think this is where our journey ends? Look at it.

Young Morgan: This has to be the place we're searching for. Mountains – fold on fold of mountains behind us to give us shelter from the cold fingers of the wind. Bushes, bright with berries – there's food for us. Water here, to drink from and to bathe in. Huge stones, cast down from these mountains, for us to build our houses with, to make shelters for our animals, to wall us in. And below us… look! This rich valley for us to grow our crops, and to see from far away the approach of enemies.

Cai: It is a good place. But… we must be sure…

Young Morgan: I am sure. I know it. It's right for us, this field.

Olwen: Please, Cai. I feel it too. This should be our home.

Cai: You are right. We belong here. I see this field is good for you, Morgan. And Elen. And Olwen. May it always be good for our people, and for all who choose to live here. Come. Let us bless this earth.

The Ever Open Door

Text 20 5C

by Ann Wade

INTRODUCTION

Before the curtain goes up we see Dr Barnardo, in his late fifties, sitting on a chair to one side of the stage. There is an empty chair next to him. A young reporter approaches. Both characters are dressed in the style of the early 1900s.

Reporter: Dr Barnardo? I'm from *The Weekly News*. I think you're expecting me…

Dr Barnardo: Sit down, sit down. You're a bit late, so we'll start at once. What did you want to know?

Reporter: Well, you're famous for the work you've been doing for years to help children. How did it all begin?

Dr Barnardo: By chance, really. I came to London from Ireland in 1866, to study medicine. I was planning to go to China, as a missionary. In the meantime, I did some preaching and teaching. And then, in about 1870, everything changed…

Reporter: What happened?

Dr Barnardo: I was teaching in a ragged school – a place where we taught the children of poor people. It was a funny sort of school – just a converted shed, really. But the children loved it. And then one evening, I had a surprise meeting with one of the pupils…

Curtain rises.
Old Dr Barnardo and the reporter sit and watch.

5D Interview with Michael Rosen — Text 21

Michael Rosen is one of the most popular of all children's poets. After enjoying a number of his poems a Junior class wrote to ask him about his work. Here are some of the answers he gave.

When did you begin writing poems?
When I was sixteen.

Where do you get your ideas from?
From things that have happened to me, and funny words or sayings.

What is your definition of a poem?
Memorable speech.

How long does it take you to write a poem?
It takes as long as it takes! You never know.

Do you cross out and make lots of changes as you write?
Yes.

What advice can you give to young writers of verse?
Write what you know about. If you're writing something true, **Don't** *Rhyme.*

Write what people really **say**. *Write what you* **think**.

Advertisement

Text 22 6A

Cornwall's Coast and Moorland

Dominated by its rocky, wave-lashed coastline, Cornwall is most renowned for its rugged cliffs and sandy coves, for its friendly harbours and beautiful creeks. Yet its attractions go deeper than its scenic splendours, for this Celtic country beyond the River Tamar is a land of legend and mystery, from the jagged heights of Tintagel to the brooding barrenness of Bodmin Moor. This is the land of King Arthur, among the greatest of Britain's legendary heroes. This is also the land of giants and piskies, of saints and smugglers, and of the lost land of Lyonnesse engulfed by the sea beyond Land's End.

All but 60 miles of Cornwall's 300-mile boundary is ocean, and most of its inland border with Devon is formed by the Tamar. The dramatic northern coastline, battered by the Atlantic, is the wildest and most rugged. The southern coast is gentler, still with steep headlands and stormy seas, but also with the creek-cut estuaries of the Helford, Fal and Fowey rivers. Inland Cornwall is mainly bleak moorland or stone-walled pastures, but even on Bodmin Moor in the north, the sea is never more than 20 miles away.

The many ruined and deserted engine-houses that bring a grim romance to the lonely cliffs are a legacy of Cornwall's [tin] mining past. Other relics are the huer's huts where lookouts once watched for the seasonal pilchard shoals, ready to signal the local fishermen to put to sea for a catch. The shoals ceased at the turn of the century, and fishing, like mining, is now only a shadow of the industry it once was.

From The Independent, 16 May, 1998

Istanbul – Where East Meets West

Istanbul is often described as the city where East meets West. It is an entirely appropriate description and one which it will keep not only for its unique geographical location, but because the city remains at the heart of Turkey's trade and commerce.

It is a staggeringly beautiful city, but also one which bustles with energy. At times the teeming population and deafening roar of traffic can overwhelm the visitor. Yet there are always quiet corners to be found and the endlessly changing views of the narrow straits of the Bosporus, one of the most crowded shipping lanes in the world, create a sense of space.

Once known as Constantinople, the city's history stretches back more than 2,500 years. It has always been an important city for trade, culture, art and politics, absorbing Christian and Moslem faiths, constantly developing its financial and educational institutions and adding to its industrial expertise.

But Istanbul's growth in the past quarter of a century has been phenomenal – to the point where overcrowding and underfunding in infrastructure, schools and welfare are throwing up serious social problems. The city's population in 1975 was 2,837,984; today the population stands at more than 9,200,000.

The Governor of Istanbul, Kutlu Aktas, says "1998 will be a better year for Istanbul." Plans to ease the horrendous traffic congestion are being tried out, and there is a masterplan for the complete reorganisation of transport in the city. Proposals include the banning of private vehicles in peak traffic areas in the city and improving public transport. Mr Aktas adds: "After the project linking the railroad and underground transport by tunnel has been completed, we will concentrate on a third bridge over the Bosporus."

Special emphasis is being placed on the construction of new hospitals and hotels, and improved health and welfare services. A start has been made on building 2,000 new classrooms to reduce the overcrowding in schools. The aim is to reduce pupil numbers from around 70 to 35 per classroom by the year 2000.

6D My Christmas Card — Text 25

Today I made a great Christmas Card at school. I sat next to John and he made one too.
We used some card (mine was cream) and some lacy paper (that was for the background). We also used lovely wrapping paper with lots of pictures on. I chose one with reindeer on, but you could use anything. We had to cut out five pictures, all the same, of the reindeer, and stick them onto thin card with glue. My fingers were aching.

While the glue was drying, I folded my card in half and stuck some lacy paper around the edges to make a border. It looked nice but the lacy bits stuck to my fingers. I wish I'd washed my hands at dinnertime now, because there were grubby marks all over the card! When everything was dry, I had to cut the reindeer out again, and now they were stiff because they were stuck on the card. I stuck the first reindeer down in the middle of the front of the card. Then I layered the reindeer directly on top of each other with a little square of card between each layer to make them stand out. I only glued them where the little bits of card were, so that there were gaps between each layer.

Lastly, I wrote a message on the inside, in pen. It was to my Grandma – I hope she likes it!

A Changing World

Text 26 6E

From "The Blue Peter Green Book" by Lewis Bronze, Nick Heathcote and Peter Brown

Riches of the Rainforest

The rainforests are scattered in a band across the Equator, but they are disappearing at an alarming rate.

Think of Aladdin's Cave, full of chests brimming with multicoloured jewels, riches beyond your wildest dreams … To someone who studies plants or insects, animals or birds, the tropical rainforests of the world are one big Aladdin's Cave. Nowhere else is there such a rich mixture of life, nowhere else contains so many secrets we have yet to discover, secrets that might cure illnesses or prevent disease, or perhaps provide new sources of food.

With so much to offer, it is an international disaster that the rainforests are being "eaten up" at such an alarming rate. Rainforests are being destroyed to make way for "civilised" man to grow crops, to provide timber, to "develop" the land. About half the world's rainforest has already gone.

We are losing species at an astonishing rate because of the destruction of the rainforests. About 50 a day, or one every half hour or so, disappears off the face of the earth forever. Each one plays some part in the balance of the rainforest.

Dolphins in danger

Dolphins, which have developed a special "friendship" with humans over the centuries, are also threatened by pollution and people. Thousands of dolphins are dying around Japan's coast as hunters cash in on the shortage of whale meat caused by the whaling ban. At least 130 000 more dolphins die each year by drowning when they get caught in tuna fishermen's nets. Greenpeace says only *urgent* action will save dolphins from extinction.

Global Warming

The average temperature of the atmosphere has risen by 0.5°C since records began in 1860. Although this may seem a very small increase, it is much faster than at any time in the past.

Most of the world's water is found in the southern hemisphere. As sea can absorb more heat than land, the impact of global warming will be felt more in the northern hemisphere. The Arctic region may become about 8°C warmer by the year 2100. The ice that melts as a result will raise global sea levels by 60–100 cm. Vast areas would be flooded. Already giant cracks in the ice have appeared and vast chunks, the size of counties, have broken off. It is estimated that a rise of 10°C would cause the Arctic region to break up. This would happen within 200 years if the present rate of warming continues.

Sweet Success

Helmann's sweet shop is celebrating its centenary in style. The family business on Danbury Road has gone from success to success since it opened exactly one hundred years ago this week.

On Saturday Mr Joseph Helmann will be giving away free chocolates to his regular customers, who have already received a special invitation. There will also be a free draw for every customer this week. The prize is a two kilogramme box of handmade chocolates.

Throughout the week Mr and Mrs Helmann will be dressed in Victorian costume, and on display will be several signs and sweet jars from when the shop first opened.

"We've quite a few other surprises too," promised Mr. Helmann mysteriously.

So if you visit Danbury Road this week then call in at Helmann's and share the taste of sweet success.

Tomboy Debbie tackles the lads!

TOMBOY Debbie Jump was banned from playing football for her Shaw school's side because teachers said it was too rough...

So the sports mad 11-year-old decided to take up rugby instead!

Now the youngster from Manor Road regularly joins the lads of Shaw's junior rugby league team and is their centre.

She started playing after watching the boys practise and one of the coaches asked her to try the game of Up and Under.

Debbie has never looked back since! She told the Advertiser: "At first the boys didn't make friends with me but when I went on to play, one of the lads started to talk to me and then all the others did."

Proud mum Pat, didn't want Debbie to play at first and refused to sign a form giving her permission for a week!

But she soon changed her mind. Said Pat: "She just loves the game, she was the first girl to play rugby league in the North West!"

Manchester United v Liverpool

These two extracts cover the same football match but in different newspapers.

From **The Sun**

DEN'N'DUSTED
Spot-king Irwin and rocket-shot Scholes KO Kop

Man Utd 2 Liverpool 0

Dennis Irwin fired United's title challenge after a disputed penalty wrecked Liverpool's hopes of breaking their Old Trafford jinx. The Republic of Ireland defender drilled in the 19th-minute spot-kick to power Alex Ferguson's side into third place in the Premiership after a bad-tempered clash that saw EIGHT booked.

Paul Scholes smashed a stunning second after 79 minutes to end Kop hopes of a comeback...

Liverpool have not won at United's Old Trafford fortress for eight years and their hopes were killed off by England star Scholes.

From **The Independent**

Scholes steals the thunder

Manchester United 2

Liverpool 0

Manchester United, so supine against Arsenal at the weekend, rediscovered their resilience if not all their verve at Old Trafford last night to defeat Liverpool and move alongside their long-standing rivals with 11 Premiership points.

In a raw rugged match of eight bookings they answered manager Alex Ferguson's demand for more fight and were rewarded with a penalty by Denis Irwin and a thunderous goal after 79 minutes from Paul Scholes...

You had to go back to 1990 for the last time Liverpool won at United, their only success at Old Trafford in their last 12 attempts.

Guy Hodgson,
25th September, 1998

The House of the Future

Janice Barker visits the Ideal Home Exhibition

I HAVE seen the house of the future – and it talked back to me. It even told me to have a nice day, reassured me about my health and personal welfare, controlled heating and water temperatures for me, looked after the finances and ordered my shopping.

It sounds fantastic – and much of it still is the product of art student minds. But just as the ice-box gave way to the deep-freeze, the brush to the vacuum cleaner and the old stove to the halogen hob, so the Vision 2020 house of the future could become a reality one day.

Sponsored by British Gas as part of the Royal College of Art's 150th anniversary, the house is a major feature of this year's Ideal Home Exhibition at Earls Court, London, which runs until April 4.

Savings

British Gas estimates that insulation levels and new energy technology in the Vision 2020 house would reduce annual gas consumption to less than a quarter of that in modern homes, and by even more in older houses.

The most simple ideas are always the best, and the RCA's students have come up trumps with the disappearing kitchen. If manufactured now, it would be an instant best-seller.

The work top, which also houses the sink, waste-disposal unit and dishwasher, is virtually seam-free and easy to clean.

The magic part is the curved, pull-out worktop and servery area which glides out from beside the kitchen unit. It has lots of storage space underneath and once the kitchen is out of use the work area slides neatly up to the kitchen unit to leave ample space in the dining area.

The stacked cooking system even includes a barbecue, and another wall houses a gas-powered refrigerator, deep-freeze, superfast freeze unit, and cool larder.

Hot or cool

A roof with insulated metal cladding and advanced double glazing in the windows and central hall area mean the heating system retains valuable heat in winter, but can also provide cool, well-ventilated rooms in summer.

A prototype domestic controller will lock all doors and windows, alert friends or neighbours if there is an emergency, and provide a complete burglar-alarm system.

In the world of the possible the house also features an electronic bathroom system. At the touch of a button, it fills the bath at the right temperature, flushes the toilet and controls the shower temperature.

There are many other features like the small but easy-to-maintain garden, and a grow cupboard – a bit like a vertical greenhouse for propagation and culture.

Unfortunately, like so much futuristic design, the word "comfort" seems to have been left out.

The atmosphere may be warm and controlled but a tiled, glass-sided hallway does not feel warm and welcoming, newly-designed cutlery hardly seems moulded to the hand, and the settee and chairs are positively uncomfortable.

You would find it hard to curl up in front of the flame-effect gas fire on the settee in this House of the Future.

The Railway Children

by E. Nesbit

They were not railway children to begin with. I don't suppose they had ever thought about the railways except as a means of getting to Makelyne and Cook's, the Pantomime, Zoological Gardens, and Madame Tussaud's. They were just ordinary suburban children, and they lived with their Father and Mother in an ordinary red-brick-fronted villa, with coloured glass in the front door, a tiled passage that was called a hall, a bathroom with hot and cold water, electric bells, French windows, a good deal of white paint, and "every modern convenience", as the house-agents say.

There were three of them. Roberta was the eldest. Of course, Mothers never have favourites, but if their Mother *had* a favourite, it might have been Roberta. Next came Peter, who wished to be an Engineer when he grew up; and the youngest was Phyllis, who meant extremely well.

Mother did not spend all her time in paying dull calls to dull ladies and sitting dully at home waiting for dull ladies to pay calls to her. She was almost always there, ready to play with the children, and read to them, and help them do their home-lessons. Besides this she used to write stories for them while they where at school, and read them aloud after tea, and she always made up funny pieces of poetry for their birthdays and for other great occasions, such as the christening of the new kittens, or the refurnishing of the doll's house, or the time when they were getting over the mumps.

These three lucky children always had everything they needed: pretty clothes, good fires, a lovely nursery with heaps of toys, and Mother Goose wall-paper. They had a kind and merry nursemaid, and a dog who was called James, and who was their very own. They also had a Father who was just perfect – never cross, never unjust, and always ready for a game – at least, if at any time he was *not* ready, he always had an excellent reason for it, and explained the reason to the children so interestingly and funnily that they felt sure he couldn't help himself.

You will think that they ought to have been very happy. And so they were, but they did not know *how* happy till the pretty life in Edgecombe Villa was over and done with, and they had to live a very different life indeed.

The dreadful change came quite suddenly.

IslandBreeze Cruises

Thomson Price Breakers, Nov 1999 April 2000

There's something happening virtually every hour of the day aboard IslandBreeze. To keep you up to speed, a copy of the Cruises News – a printed programme for the next day's activities – will be popped under your cabin door daily. A typical day at sea might start with a gentle stretch-and-tone session on the Sun Deck; once you're limbered up, you could learn to Nashville line-dance with one of the ship's dancers. We'll make sure you know your way around the extensive equipment in the IslandBreeze's gym, and that you don't get distracted by the unique view (you'll have to see it to appreciate it!). There's no special training needed for the traditional deck sports like shuffleboard, just a keen eye, steady hand, and good sense of humour. But no one will scold if you simply stretch out and apply sunblock and a good book from the library to your nose. After lunch you might be tempted to move indoors, where a host of activities are under way around the ship. There's a bridge tournament in the handsomely furnished Library/Card Room and a bingo session in one of the bars. The band's pianist challenges your ear with Name That Tune, while the Head Barman might be leading a 'mix-master' class (be sure to sample the ship's own speciality cocktails).

Choose Your Cabin

All IslandBreeze cabins are fully air-conditioned and have a fitted wardrobe, drawers, wall-to-wall carpeting, and en-suite facilities (shower, wc and hand-basin).

☼ Superior

Superior class lets you enjoy your cruise on a higher deck, and generally in more spacious surroundings. A number of both inside and outside cabins have a third or fourth berth, making them most appealing to families. Some cabins with double beds are also available. Outside cabins all have a picture window or porthole. (Please note: the view from some Superior Outside cabins on the Verandah deck are fully or partially obstructed.)

☼ Standard

All Standard cabins are tastefully furnished, with two lower beds; outside cabins have a porthole. Some cabins with a third and fourth upper berth are also available, and the IslandBreeze has quite a few cabins with double beds.

☼ Two-berths

Two berth cabins are great value-for-money if you don't plan on spending a lot of time in your cabin. Space for storage is limited; one bed is always an upper berth that folds down from the wall. Please note: cots are not permitted in two berth cabins. Aboard the IslandBreeze, wash-basins in some cabins are set in a vanity unit between the two beds.

You're back on board from your excursion ashore; you've met friends for a relaxing sun-downer at The Pub; now you're ready for a delicious dinner and night 'on the town'. There's a fabulous musical revue on in the Piccadilly Theatre and a dance band playing in the Cordoba Lounge. The wheels of fortune are spinning in the Monte Carlo Casino, and a quiet duo warming up in the Portofino Lounge. But best of all there's a full moon shining on the deck – an irresistible invitation to have a night-cap at the Capri Bar.

Day One – Friday **Tenerife** Port: Santa Cruz
We sail late evening.
Day Two – Saturday **Gran Canaria**
Port: Las Palmas
Day Three – Sunday **Lanzarote**
Port: Playa Blanca*
Day Four – Monday **Morocco** Port: Agadir
Day Five – Tuesday **Morocco** Port: Casablanca
Day Six – Wednesday **At Sea**
Day Seven – Thursday **Madeira** Port: Funchal
Day Eight – Friday **Tenerife** Port: Santa Cruz

Disembark after breakfast for your transfer to your hotel in Tenerife.

*Tender to shore

Frogs and Toads

by Trevor Beebee

Frogs on Roads

The annual carnage of toads migrating to their breeding ponds, run over by traffic on roads they have to cross, has not been ignored by naturalists and conservationalists. 'Toads on roads' campaigns of various sorts have been tried in Britain and elsewhere, and usually at least one rescue operation features on the TV each spring. Several remedies have been attempted. The simplest involves a team of volunteers manning the point where toads cross the road for the several days and nights of peak migration, collecting them up as they arrive and carrying them to the other side. Some places even have special road signs depicting a toad, unfolded at the key time, warning drivers to motor carefully over the coming section of road. More elaborate ideas include toad 'tunnels' under the roads, rather like those provided for badgers on some motorways; the design has to be just right before toads will use them, though, and they are expensive to install. Another idea is to put a toad-proof fence parallel to the road, with buckets set into the ground at intervals along it. Toads coming to the fence wander along trying to get round, fall into a bucket and are collected for carriage across the road early each day.

All of these methods can work fairly well, but it's much more difficult helping the toads get back again when they have finished breeding because they leave the pond area in dribs and drabs over a long period of time. And the toadlets must have an even worse problem in mid-summer; no one seems to have thought much about them. Scientific studies have indicated that toad road deaths are unlikely to pose a serious threat to a population, though they look, and indeed are, horrific spectacles. Whether or not there is a sound conservation case for helping toad jaywalkers, there clearly is a compassionate one. County naturalists trusts, the British Herpetological Society and others carry out these rescues, which are also excellent ways of encouraging communities to become involved with their local toad ponds – the soundest possible base for conservation.

Toad in a Hole

There used to be a popular myth that toads can live for years entombed in a block of stone. Probably this originated with animals being found by quarrymen who didn't look too closely for holes where the toads might have crept in, but the story prompted one of the earliest ever herpetological experiments by Dean Buckland back in the 1820s. He actually walled-up living toads in cells cut in wood or stone, and then watched what happened. Of course the outcome would be obvious to any present-day naturalist, but in those times it was novel. Inevitably the toads within properly sealed cells died within a few months, but any small cracks in the walls or covers allowed the poor creatures to survive a year or two. Presumably a few insects crept in and were just enough to sustain the toads, and it's possible to imagine a tiny toad entering a natural cell through a small crack, growing too big to get out, and being trapped there for the rest of its life. Possible, but pretty unlikely, since toads usually emerge from their hiding places every night to hunt and would surely abandon a home with a small entrance when they couldn't get back in again.

THE ANURAN YEAR

JANUARY Hibernating, but wake for short spells if the temperature rises.	FEBRUARY Many still hibernating, but frogs tend to move off to their breeding ponds.	MARCH Early March: toads migrate *en masse* to breeding ponds and frogs spawn. Late March: toads spawn, some natterjacks migrate, and some frog tadpoles hatch.	APRIL Natterjacks spawn. Frog and toad tadpoles hatch and grow. Adult toads leave the ponds. 
MAY Natterjacks continue to spawn. Metamorphosis of early frog and some toad tadpoles. Adult frogs leave the ponds. 	JUNE Young frog and toadlets leave the ponds. A few natterjacks still spawning. 	JULY Adult frogs live in long grass. Remaining natterjack tadpoles undergo metamorphosis and any remaining froglets leave the water. 	AUGUST Late natterjack toadlets leave the water. 
SEPTEMBER All young animals eat greedily to gain body reserves for winter. 	OCTOBER Hibernation begins as the weather becomes cooler, male frogs under water and all others on land. 	NOVEMBER Hibernating, but wake occasionally. Some young animals may still be hunting. Natterjacks burrow into sand or use existing holes. 	DECEMBER Hibernating, but wake to feed in warm weather for short periods.